Edinburgh Pocket Guide

Iseabail Macleod

Colin Baxter Photography Limited, Grantown-on-Spey, Scotland

First published in Great Britain in 1996 by
Colin Baxter Photography Ltd, Grantown-on-Spey, Moray, Scotland

Reprinted 1997, 1998
Revised edition 2001

Text Copyright © Iseabail Macleod 1996, 2001
Photographs Copyright © Colin Baxter 1996, 2001
Maps © The XYZ Digital Map Co. 2001
All rights reserved

www.colinbaxter.co.uk

A CIP catalogue record for this book is available from the British Library
ISBN 1 84107 077 7

Printed in China

Edinburgh Pocket Guide

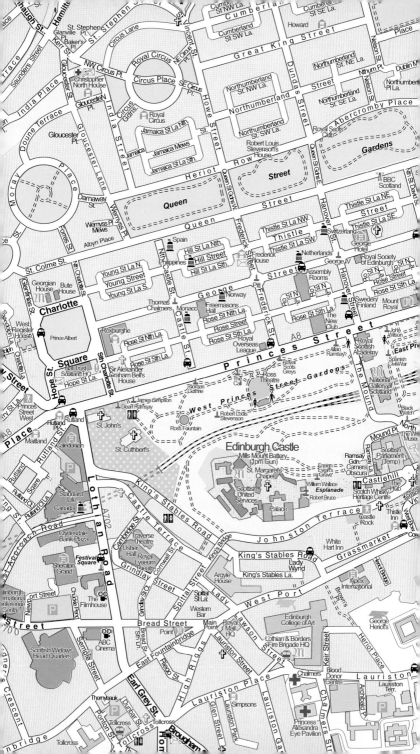

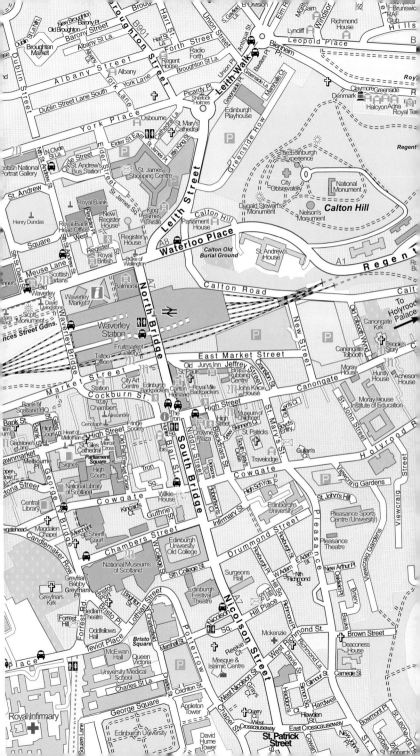

INTRODUCTION

Edinburgh is a city with a wealth of striking features, natural and man-made. Its site on the Firth of Forth makes it in effect a seaside town and it is built on more hills than Rome. The most prominent of these are the Castle Rock and Arthur's Seat, both of them with evidence of use as forts back to prehistoric times. It is a city of long vistas of hill, sea, street and wood, some of them opening out in the most unexpected places, as you turn a corner or breast a hill: as you reach George Street for example, the River Forth and the hills of Fife beyond suddenly appear below you; as you descend the Royal Mile, the sea can be seen in the distance beyond the towering tenements. And the Castle appears majestically from many different angles. As well as the remaining medieval buildings of the Old Town, Edinburgh has some of the finest Georgian architecture anywhere.

This little book attempts to give you a brief outline of the city centre, what you can see, what to do there, and how to find your way around.

History

It is not difficult to see why there should have been settlements here since the earliest times, and at least since the 11th century Edinburgh has been a centre of some importance in Scotland, with the Castle and later Holyrood Abbey providing residences for the Kings of Scots, though it did not become officially the capital of Scotland until the 17th century. It witnessed the turbulent times of the 14th-century Wars of Independence and later struggles against England, the Reformation in 1560 and the troubled reign of Mary, Queen of Scots, the Union of the Crowns with England under her son, James VI, in 1603, and in 1707 the Treaty of Union with England, when the Scottish Parliament joined with that of England to form the United Kingdom.

These latter events robbed Edinburgh of a great deal of its status as a capital city but certain areas of Scottish life retained their independence, notably the legal system, the church and education, and all of these are prominent in Edinburgh today. The new Scottish Parliament, opened in July 1999, has however brought back increased power to the city and with it a new atmosphere of cultural revival and awareness of Scottish identity. Edinburgh is the centre of Scotland's legal system, which is radically different from that of England and Wales, and the home of its two supreme courts (see also pp.24 and

25). Edinburgh witnessed the turmoils of the Reformation and the religious strife of the 17th century when the Covenanters struggled for the right to worship in their chosen Presbyterian fashion against successive attempts to enforce an episcopal system. The Presbyterian system survived in the Church of Scotland but over the years many splits took place, producing new sects and groupings. The most important of these was the Disruption in 1843, when 474 ministers walked out of the Church of Scotland's General Assembly to form the Free Church of Scotland, in which they could make their own choice of ministers.

Scotland has always valued education highly and this too is strongly in evidence in Edinburgh where there are now three universities as well as several colleges of higher education. Since the 17th century, many bequests have been left to the city for the foundation of schools and orphanages and many of these schools are still in existence, some under the aegis of the Merchant Company (Daniel Stewart's & Melville College, George Watson's, Mary Erskine's). James Gillespie's has now been absorbed into the state system, but in its private days, it was the prototype of St Marcia's in Muriel Spark's *The Prime of Miss Jean Brodie*.

The medieval city was clustered along the ridge of the hill descending from the Castle Rock (see p.12) but by the 18th century expansion became necessary and the New Town was built to the north (see p.38). This period saw a flowering not only architecturally but also intellectually in the remarkable brilliance of the Scottish Enlightenment. Among its giants were the philosopher David Hume, the economist and philospher Adam Smith, the philospher Adam Fergusson, the historian William Robertson, and the (medical) scientists William Cullen and Joseph Black. Literary Edinburgh flourished, especially in the early 19th century with the genius of Sir Walter Scott, and the pre-eminence of the *Edinburgh Review* and other literary magazines.

The book industry had many representatives here, and indeed in comparatively recent times Edinburgh was known for the three 'B's: beer, books, and banking, but with the decline of the manufacturing industry, only the third plays a major role in today's economy. Money is indeed prominent, with many banks, insurance companies and other financial institutions having their headquarters here. As well as the legal and educational establishments, government departments and local government provide employment for many and tourism has increasing importance.

Approaches to Edinburgh

Many travellers today arrive in Edinburgh by air, crossing the Firth of Forth from the south and circling over the coast of Fife to descend into Edinburgh Airport on the west side of the city. The route into the city passes the Royal Highland Showground at Ingliston, before joining the main road from Glasgow and the West. Recent developments have improved its linkage with the City Bypass, which carries traffic round the southern periphery of the city, part of its route along the foot of the Pentland Hills. The route into the centre passes Corstorphine Hill and Edinburgh Zoo and soon the Castle on its high rock looms ahead, with Arthur's Seat as backdrop. The large imposing building on the left near the centre, however, is not a Jacobean palace, but a 19th-century orphanage (Donaldson's School for the Deaf, see p.64).

Approach from the north, by road or rail, usually involves crossing one of the great bridges across the Forth, the gigantic shape of the 1890s railway bridge contrasting with the more delicate suspension structure of the road bridge, opened in 1964. Routes from the south vary, with the A1 coming in from the east and the A68 more directly from the south through the Border country. Many people today, however, prefer to travel up the M6, A74, M74 and then along the M8 and A8 from the west as described above.

Railway journeys today usually end at Edinburgh's one mainline terminus, Waverley Station, bringing the tourist right into the heart of the capital.

Festivals

In 1947 the first Edinburgh International Festival brought music and drama of a high order to a culture-starved postwar world. It has taken place in August/September annually since. Its most spectacular event is the Edinburgh Military Tattoo on the Castle Esplanade. Gradually events on the 'fringe' of the main Festival grew in number until today the Edinburgh Festival Fringe is one of the largest theatrical events in the world. Other festivals have grown up around these; the Edinburgh International Film Festival also takes place in August as does the Edinburgh International Book Festival. They are preceded by the Edinburgh International Jazz Festival early in August and in the spring the Edinburgh Folk Festival (March-April) is followed by the Edinburgh International Science Festival. The new year is now celebrated with Edinburgh's Hogmanay, a gigantic street party, with music, fireworks and processions.

THE OLD TOWN

Medieval Edinburgh clustered along a steep ridge, the result of a glacial feature known to geologists as crag and tail; the crag is the Castle Rock, the remains of an old volcano, and the tail is the ridge which descends to Holyrood Abbey. The growth of the Old Town was thus limited by geographical

The many-chimneyed roofs remind us of heating methods of another age, which gave Edinburgh the nickname of Auld Reekie (old smoky).

factors. After severe overcrowding had compelled expansion to the New Town in the 18th century (see p. 38), there was considerable redevelopment in the 19th, continuing to the present day. There remain however many reminders of the bustling medieval city and, owing to the complex old struc-tures on the very steep slope, many more are still to be found underground (lending a mysterious atmosphere for the many ghost tours which are now a major tourist attraction!)

In 1999, the upper, western end of the Old Town became a temporary home for the new Scottish Parliament, with a debating chamber in the Assembly Hall on the Mound (see pp. 22 and 32).

THE ROYAL MILE

The main street of the Old Town has been so called since the 16th century because its mile length joins the two main residences of the medieval Kings of Scots, the Castle (see p.14) and the more congenial Holyrood Palace (see p.31). The Royal Mile consists of Castlehill, the Lawnmarket (meaning the land market, where produce from the surrounding countryside was sold), the High Street and the Canongate. The last two were divided until 1764 by the Netherbow Port (see p.27), marking the boundary of the city with that of the burgh of Canongate, which remained a separate town until 1856. The Royal Mile is the backbone of the Old Town of Edinburgh, forming the crest of the ridge.

The Royal Mile from the Outlook Tower, sweeping downhill towards Holyrood.

Early buildings fronted onto the street but building had to be extended into courtyards behind; access to buildings further back was, and is, through pends (archways) or by closes or wynds, narrow passageways which often take their names from former occupants of the buildings, for example Brodie's Close (see p.22), Advocate's Close (named for an early 18th-century Lord Advocate); some, such as Old Fishmarket Close, take their names from the trades carried on in or near them.

The steep slopes meant very restricted space, and buildings went upwards from an early date, there being houses of ten storeys and more in medieval times, many of these below the street level of the frontage. They are often referred to as tenements or lands (originally referring to the holdings on which they were built – see Gladstone's Land p.21). Although few medieval

The Edinburgh Military Tattoo on the Castle Esplanade takes place every year during the Edinburgh International Festival.

buildings remain (a large number of today's date from the 19th century), the general pattern survives. The high density inevitably led to serious overcrowding by the 18th century, an interesting result of which was the mixture of social classes, with aristocrats and judges often sharing a stair with artisans and paupers. The sanitary conditions were appalling; the cry from an upper window of 'Gardy loo' (French *garde à l'eau* meaning beware of the water) was at once a euphemism and a dire warning. By the middle of the century new developments became essential (see New Town p.38).

Edinburgh Castle: Though its individual buildings are not on the whole architecturally distinguished, the Castle on its naturally fortified Rock site forms a magnificent backdrop to Old Town and New Town alike. With springs which supplied water and enough grazing for cattle nearby, it was an obvious place for a fortress from ancient times. Recent excavations have produced evidence of occupation going back to about 850 BC, including Iron-Age and Dark-Age forts. It first appears in written history in the 11th century as the home of King Malcolm III (Malcolm Canmore) and his English Queen Margaret, and from that time it became a frequent home of the medieval Kings of Scots. It was also used for councils and assemblies and as a treasury and record store.

It suffered damage in the 14th century, especially in the Wars of Independence against England. In 1314 it was recaptured from the English by a daring climb up the Castle Rock by Sir Thomas Randolph, Earl of Moray, nephew of King Robert the Bruce. In 1573 it was held for Mary, Queen of Scots, in what became known as the Lang Siege, by Sir William Kirkcaldy of Grange against the supporters of her son James VI. It received further batterings and occupations during the troubled times of the 17th century and the Jacobite risings of the 18th, the last (unsuccessful) siege being by the troops of Prince Charles Edward Stuart in 1745.

Though no longer used as a military barracks, the Castle does house a unit of the Military Police and various Divisional officers. **The National War Museum of Scotland**, opened in 2000, tells the story of Scottish involvement in war and military service. Six theme-based galleries are housed in the 18th-century former hospital block on the west side. At a higher level, in Crown Square, is the Scottish National War Memorial (1927 Robert Lorimer), containing the names of the dead of two World Wars. On the south side of the Square is the **Great Hall**, dating in its present form from the early 16th century, with much restoration in the late 19th. Its hammerbeam roof has carved masks, human and animal, at the ends of the beams, as well as carved stone corbels. The Hall has had many uses over the centuries, including times as a barracks and as a hospital, but it is now once more used on ceremonial occasions, such as official banquets.

The **Palace**, on the east side, dates from the 15th century, with later additions. On the first floor is the **Crown Room**, where the Scottish regalia, the Crown, Sceptre and Sword of State, can be seen. During Cromwell's time the Crown (of Scottish gold) was moved for safety to Dunnottar Castle on the north-east coast. When that too was besieged it was smuggled out to be hidden by the wife of a local minister and thus survived. At the Union of the Parliaments in 1707 the regalia were sealed into their strong-room in the Castle. There they remained until 1818 when Sir Walter Scott secured a royal warrant to open the sealed vault. The regalia have recently been joined by the Stone of Destiny, returned to Scotland from Westminster Abbey; it was removed from Scone Abbey by Edward I in 1296. Adjoining rooms contain models and displays illustrating Scottish history and events in the castle. In the royal apartments on the ground floor is the tiny panelled Queen Mary's Room, where Mary, Queen of Scots gave birth to the future James VI in 1566.

The Castle's oldest building is the Norman **St Margaret's Chapel**, dating with many restorations from the 12th century. Although for centuries it was believed to have been the private chapel of Queen Margaret, it was more probably built in her memory by her son David I. Services are still held in it occasionally, for army weddings and baptisms.

The **Half-Moon Battery** to the east was built by Regent Morton in 1574, partly on the ruin of the 14th-century **David's Tower**, which dates from the rebuilding of the Castle (1367-77) in the reign of David II. It was destroyed during the Lang Siege of 1573.

The Castle's most famous piece of artillery is the 15th-century cannon Mons Meg; though legend gives it a Scottish origin, it was probably manufactured in Flanders. It is now to be found in the vaults of the Castle, which were formerly used as a prison; French (naval) prisoners of war were held

here between 1756 and 1815.

The Castle is now well supplied with shops and cafés, including a restaurant in a new building overlooking the ramparts, with a splendid view to the north. The Officers' Mess is housed in the elegant 18th-century **Governor's House** opposite.

The **Esplanade** was built in the early 19th century as a parade ground and it is now used for various ceremonies and entertainments, the most spectacular being the annual Edinburgh Military Tattoo during the Edinburgh International Festival in August/September.

The **One o'Clock Gun** has been fired from the Castle ramparts every week-day at 1pm since 1861.

The highest area of the Castle is approached by Foog's Gate.

It was originally used as a time signal for shipping on the Forth but now serves to distinguish tourists from residents: the former jump out of their skins in surprise, the latter look at their watches.

Ramsay Garden: This row of 18th- and 19th-century houses below the Castle Esplanade takes its name from the poet Allan Ramsay, father of the portrait painter. His octagonal house is included at the western end.

Tartan Weaving Mill and Exhibition: A new exhibition and shop are housed in the former Castlehill Reservoir, just below the Castle esplanade. It was first built in 1681 to supply clean drinking water to the Old Town.

Cannonball House: An early 17th-century merchant's house, it derives its nickname from a cannonball embedded in the west gable. A dormer window bears the date 1630 and the initials AM MN (of Alex Mure, an Edinburgh furrier, and his wife).

Ramsay Garden – pleasant living within a few metres of the Castle.

Scotch Whisky Heritage Centre: An imaginative audio-visual exhibition displaying both the history and the making of Scotch whisky.

Boswell's Court: This is a 17th-century tenement, named after an uncle of James Boswell, biographer of Dr Johnson.

The Hub: The Edinburgh International Festival's headquarters just below the Castle now form an exciting new Festival Centre in a

19th-century Gothic church. The Tolbooth St John's Church (1842-44, James Gillespie Graham) was constructed for the General Assembly of the Church of Scotland as well as for the congregation of the old Tolbooth Kirk. More recently it was the Church of Scotland's main Gaelic church in the city.

Camera Obscura/Outlook Tower: This dark-topped white tower, so conspicuous on the Old Town skyline, houses the Camera Obscura, a system of revolving lenses and mirrors which gives a panoramic view of the city. (On a clear day the view from the roof is also stunning.) When it was installed in the 1850s, the 17th-century building was extended upwards to provide the necessary height. Today various exhibitions, including one of holography, accompany the Camera Obscura. In the 1890s it was bought by Sir Patrick Geddes for use as the 'world's first sociological laboratory'; he was a pioneer of town planning.

Over the roofs and towers of the Old Town, Calton Hill appears, with the Firth of Forth beyond.

Ensign Ewart's pub: This public house commemorates the sergeant of the Scots Greys who captured the eagle standard of the French 45th regiment at the Battle of Waterloo in 1815.

Mylne's Court: Designed in 1690 by Robert Mylne (see also Palace of Holyroodhouse p.31), this was an early example of slum clearance and courtyard planning in the old Edinburgh. In the 1960s it was restored and converted to a hall of residence for Edinburgh University.

Deacon Brodie's Tavern – one of the many Royal Mile pubs with historical associations. Brodie was a respected councillor by day, and a practised thief by night.

James' Court (1723-7 James Brownhill): Again old tenements were removed to form a courtyard of upper-class dwellings. The philosopher David Hume lived here for a time, and later James Boswell; he entertained Samuel Johnson here in 1773 en route for their Hebridean tour. In 1857 the massive double tenement to the north (looking onto the Mound) was badly damaged by fire and the western section was restored to form the Free Church of Scotland College and Offices (1858-60 David Cousin), largely in 17th-century style but retaining some 18th-century parts; the adjoining tenement remains in its 18th-century form, but it was reconstructed internally in the 1980s for use as flats.

Gladstone's Land: A 16th-century house was much extended in the early 17th by an Edinburgh burgess, Thomas Gledstanes. Now owned by the National Trust for Scotland, it is a fine example of a building of its day and is furnished in the style of the period. It is open to the public (with NTS shop and a reconstruction of a 17th-century shop on the ground floor). Characteristic features are the outside staircase to the first floor and splendid painted ceilings and other decoration in the front rooms.

Gladstone's Land, one of the best-preserved older buildings in the Lawnmarket.

Riddell's Court: This was originally built in the 1590s as a mansion for Bailie John Macmorran, a wealthy Edinburgh merchant (whose life ended rather dramatically when he was shot by a schoolboy during a school riot). In this house in 1598 the Town Council held a banquet for James VI and his Queen, Anne of Denmark, and visiting members of the Danish court. The courtyard was restored in 1893 and again in 1964; at present it is used as a local-authority educational centre.

Writers' Museum: A literary museum with interesting relics of three of Scotland's greatest writers, Robert Burns, Sir Walter Scott and Robert Louis Stevenson. Formerly known as Lady Stair's House, the building is a 19th-century re-creation of a 17th-century house; in the early 18th century it belonged to Lady Stair, wife of the 2nd Earl of Stair.

(Her romantic story can be read in *Traditions of Edinburgh* by Robert Chambers.) Recently quotations from Scottish writers through the ages have been engraved in the flagstones of the courtyard.

Assembly Hall/New College (1846-50 William Playfair): The two square towers of the gatehouse dominate the Mound below, and the quadrangle behind is crowned by two octagonal towers above the Lawnmarket. As well as the meeting place of the General Assembly of the Church of Scotland, the complex contains New College where its ministers and other students of theology study. In recent years the apron stage of the Assembly Hall has been used for many spectacular dramatic performances at the Edinburgh Festival. In 1999 it became a temporary debating chamber for the Scottish Parliament (see p. 32).

Brodie's Close: Though dating from the 16th century, this lane takes its present name from a later owner, the father of Deacon Brodie; the latter was famous in the 18th century for his double life, as a respectable craftsman and town councillor by day and as the leader of a gang of burglars by night. Not only the subject of a play by R L Stevenson, he was a large element of his inspiration for *Dr Jekyll and Mr Hyde*. Brodie is also commemorated in **Deacon Brodie's Tavern** on the corner of Bank Street, where he is portrayed hanging from the gibbet, the first victim of a new style of gibbet which he himself had invented. (See also Chessels Court p.27).

Bank of Scotland (1802-06 Robert Reid and Richard Crichton, extended 1865-70 David Bryce): With a commanding position at the head of the Mound, the Bank's headquarters combine the classical features of the original building with the more florid style of the later Victorian parts.

St Giles' Cathedral: With its crown tower the cathedral is one of the most prominent landmarks on Edinburgh's skyline. Strictly, the High Kirk of Edinburgh, it was officially a cathedral only for two brief periods in the 17th century when attempts were being made to impose an episcopal order on the Scottish church. There may have been a church on this site since the 9th century and there are some remnants from as far back as the 12th, but the main structure of the present building dates from the 14th and 15th centuries. After the Reformation in 1560 all altars and ornaments

were removed. John Knox, the Scottish reformer, became its first Protestant minister. A modern statue of him can be seen near the west door.

St Giles' was divided into several churches and it became crowded in by other buildings, including the **Old** and **New Tolbooths**, latterly the town jail, and the rows of timber-fronted tenements to the north along the High Street. These were known as the Luckenbooths, meaning 'lockable shops', from the shops on the ground floor. These were all demolished by 1817 and the building was then seen to be in a deplorable state; necessary restoration by William Burn in the 1820s produced the Georgian stonework of today's exterior and

The Old Town floodlit at dusk, with the crown tower of St Giles' rising above.

only the tower retains its medieval stonework. Further restoration, financed largely by the publisher William Chambers (see Chambers Street, p.53), especially of the interior, took place in the late 19th century, restoring the unity of the building. Recent developments include the creation below the church of a series of rooms, some of them medieval in origin, which are used as a restaurant.

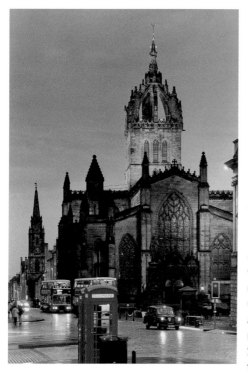

Most of the stained glass dates from the 19th century but the great west window was dedicated in 1985 as a tribute to Scotland's greatest poet, Robert Burns; it was designed by the Icelandic artist Leifur Breidfjord. A magnificent modern organ was installed in 1992 (built by Rieger Orgelbau of Austria and funded by a member of the Salvesen family). To the south-east is the

The front facade of St Giles', in medieval Gothic style.

Thistle Chapel (1911 Robert Lorimer), in highly ornate Gothic style. The Order of the Thistle is Scotland's highest order of chivalry and has 16 knights as well as royal members.

Parliament Hall: The Renaissance building of the old Scottish parliament received a new Georgian facade in the early 19th century, though much of the interior remains. Today it is the hub of the legal profession: as well as chambers for law lords and advocates (barristers), it houses Scotland's supreme courts, the Court of Session (civil) and the High Court (of Justiciary) (criminal). The hall itself, with its hammerbeam roof, is still in use by lawyers and their clients. The courts are open to the public. In the square outside is a late 17th-century equestrian statue of Charles II in the garb of a Roman emperor. The High Court now holds trials in the former Sheriff Courthouse (1934-7) across the street.

Heart of Midlothian: In the middle of Parliament Square, to the north-west of St Giles', a heart shape worked into the cobbled street marks the site of the Old Tolbooth of Edinburgh; originally a Council house, it later became the town's main prison (demolished in 1817). Presumably in memory of its latter use, the heart is frequently spat on by passers-by. Oblong metal markings in the roadway indicate the precise site of the building and its various extensions. Its nickname was made famous by Sir Walter Scott's novel and is now best known as the name of one of the city's two main football teams (often shortened to Hearts or, in rhyming slang, Jam Tarts). Nearby is a statue of the 5th Duke of Buccleuch who built the pier and breakwater at Granton harbour on the Forth in the 1830s.

On the other side of St Giles' is the **Mercat Cross**, from which proclamations were made (and indeed still are on royal occasions). Knocked down in the 18th century the cross was re-erected in 1885, in a smaller altered form, and restored with a new shaft in 1970.

City Chambers (1753-61 John Fergus, on basis of a design by John Adam): Originally built as the Royal Exchange and later (1811) adapted for Council use. Below there remain many storeys of older buildings, including **Mary King's Close**, a street said to have been deserted after an outbreak of plague there in the mid 17th century.

Edinburgh Festival Fringe offices, on the opposite side, enliven the street with their brightly coloured statues.

Tron Church (1636-47 John Mylne): Built originally for the congregation which had to be moved when St Giles' became a cathedral, it was reconstructed in the late 18th century and a new and higher tower was added in 1829 (after the disastrous fire of 1824, which gutted many buildings in the Old Town). Its fine Renaissance roof survives. Out of use as a church since 1952, its gutted interior is currently used for exhibitions. Building work in recent decades has revealed traces of a medieval street, Marlin's Wynd, and the adjacent buildings. The name Tron comes from Scots 'tron', a public weighing machine, often one in a marketplace and thus forming a focal point in an area. One such was situated near here, and to this day New Year revellers gather round the church on Hogmanay (New Year's Eve).

The Festival Fringe office at 180 High St on the Royal Mile with sculptures designed by Gerald Scarfe.

Crowne Plaza (1989 Ian Begg) – formerly Scandic Crown Hotel: A hotel in medieval Scottish style.

Museum of Childhood (see p.73): This museum contains not only toys, but all kinds of objects connected with childhood in the past.

Tweeddale Court: Originally the home of the Marquis of Tweeddale and built in the 16th century with later additons, this courtyard was for many years the home of Oliver & Boyd, well-known Edinburgh publishers. Recent restoration has brought the book world back to it, with other publishing offices. To the back of the courtyard is the Saltire Society, a pressure group for Scottish culture.

John Knox House: This projects into the High

Street with its timbered south facade. It is not certain whether the Scottish religious leader actually lived in this building but the upper parts of it do date from the 16th century (the initials IM and MA on the coat of arms stand for (in Latin) James Mossman, goldsmith to Mary, Queen of Scots, and his wife Mariota Arres, who inherited it in 1556). It is open to the public and now forms

part of the **Netherbow Arts Centre**, comprising small theatre, gallery space, café, in a modern building which stands at the site of the Netherbow Port. This city gate dated from medieval times and was demolished in 1764 to improve traffic flow.

John Knox House, one of the few medieval buildings left above ground in the Royal Mile.

Brass-rubbing Centre/Trinity Apse: Open to the public for brass-rubbing, is housed in the reconstructed remains of Trinity College Church, a splendid 15th-century building, which stood below the Calton Hill; it was demolished in 1848 to make way for railway development.

Chessels Court: This is a good example of the many courtyards along the Royal Mile. To the rear is an elegant block of flats originally built about

1745 and recently restored. In this courtyard was the excise office where Deacon Brodie was finally caught (see p.22).

The area now has some very pleasant housing and office buildings, some new and some restored, and there are plans to open up more of the closes, giving easier access from the Canongate to new developments in Holyrood Road (see p.32).

Moray House: A mansion-house built about 1625 by Mary, Dowager Countess of Home (and named for her daughter, Margaret, Countess of Moray), it became part of Moray House College of Education (now the Faculty of Education, University of Edinburgh).

Canongate Tolbooth: This late 16th-century building was the town house of the burgh of Canongate (meaning 'road of the Canons': the Canons of the Abbey of Holyroodhouse were granted the right to create their own burgh and it remained separate from Edinburgh until 1856). An outside stair leads up to the first-floor council chamber, where there is now **'The People's Story',** a museum of life in the city. **The Tolbooth Tavern** on the ground floor dates from 1820.

Canongate Tolbooth, now a museum, reminds us that Canongate was once an independent town.

Huntly House Museum (see also p.73): This 16th-century building was extended in the late 17th century by two timber-framed storeys. It was restored in the 1920s to form a museum. It is now a local-history museum, containing varied objects connected with Edinburgh's past industries, as well as restored interior features, both from its own past and from other buildings.

Acheson House: Just below Huntly House, but set back from the street, is an early 17th-century house built for Sir Archibald Acheson, Secretary of

State. It was restored in the 1930s for the Marquess of Bute.

Canongate Kirk: When in 1687 James VII had the nave of Holyrood Abbey converted into a chapel for the Order of the Thistle, a new church was built, to a design by James Smith, for the parish of Canongate. Opened in 1691, it has a pleasingly simple cruciform shape. It is surrounded by the Canongate Kirkyard, with many tombs notable for their design as well as for their occupants, who include the poet Robert Fergusson (d. 1774, his headstone erected by fellow-poet Robert Burns) and the economist and philosopher Adam Smith (d. 1791).

The royal arms on the facade of Canongate Kirk, built by order of King James VII.

The Scottish Poetry Library has moved to an interesting modern building, in Crighton's Close, just off the Canongate, close to the site of the new Scottish Parliament building. It has reference and lending facilities for Scottish and international poetry.

Set back in a courtyard on the opposite side of the street is **Whitefoord House** (1769 Robert

Whitehorse Close at the foot of the Royal Mile, with its restored 17th-century buildings.

Mylne), a three-storey building, now a home for ex-servicemen.

Whitehorse Close: One of the most picturesque courtyards in the Royal Mile, its 17th-century buildings, formerly White Horse Inn, have undergone restoration twice in the last century or so. In the 18th century it was the starting point for the stagecoaches to London, a journey originally lasting 10 to 12 days, though much speeded up as time went on.

Queen Mary's Bath-house: This is the name given to a small, oddly-shaped 16th-century building near the north gate of the Palace. No one seems to be quite sure how it got its equally odd name or what its original purpose really was.

Abbey Strand: This little corner at the bottom of the Royal Mile contains a four-storey 16th-century mansion to the west and a later two-storey house to the east, known as Lucky Spence's house. ('Lucky' is a Scots word for an old woman, often a tavern-owner; Lucky Spence was a woman of doubtful character, who lived in the

18th century, immortalized in a rather bawdy poem by Allan Ramsay).

Abbey of Holyroodhouse: Founded by David I in 1128, the ruined remains date mainly from the 13th century. In the 17th century the nave became the Chapel Royal and later Chapel of the Order of the Thistle (see Canongate Kirk and St Giles' Cathedral, pp.29 and 24). In 1768 the roof collapsed, a few years after an injudicious attempt to repair it with stone slabs.

Palace of Holyroodhouse: In the later Middle Ages the Kings of Scots used the Abbey as a residence and in 1501 a new palace was begun by James IV, just prior to his marriage to

Holyrood Palace from the air, showing clearly the 16th-century tower on the left, and the 17th-century quadrangle.

Margaret Tudor. It was extended by James V about 1530 and the present north-west tower dates from that time. Further extensions were made over the years but much damage was done in 1650 by a fire during its occupation by Cromwell's troops. After the Restoration in 1660 plans were set afoot to extend the Palace and it thus acquired its present form to a design by William Bruce, the King's Surveyor, along with Robert Mylne, the King's Master Mason (see p.20). Bruce balanced the 16th-century tower with another to the south and joined and extended them into an impressive quadrangle. The historic apartments are open to the public. A new use has been found, as a regional office for Historic Scotland, for one of the oldest buildings in the area, **Croft-an-Righ**, an early 17th-century house behind the Palace.

Holyrood – a changing landscape: There was brewing in the areas around Holyrood Abbey from the early Middle Ages, when the monks of the Abbey made ale from the clear water of the wells in the district, until 1986 when Scottish and Newcastle closed the last brewery. Massive changes are taking place. The most important of these is the choice of this area for the home of the new **Scottish Parliament.**

A large part of the site was the former headquarters of Scottish and Newcastle brewers. It also includes **Queensberry House**, an impressive late 17th-century building on the Canongate, which has seen many changes of use, most recently as a geriatric hospital. In spite of its poor state of repair, it is planned to incorporate it into the Parliament complex. It is hoped that the Parliament will move to its permanent site in 2002.

Other new developments have changed the atmosphere on the edge of the Royal Park, notably **Our Dynamic Earth**, a spectacular tent-like structure in Holyrood Road, in which the story of the earth is dramatically told using the latest technology.

GEORGE IV BRIDGE, GRASSMARKET, COWGATE

National Library of Scotland: This grew out of the Advocate's Library, founded for the legal profession in the late 17th century. It was housed in Parliament House and other legal buildings until the new building was opened in 1956. The plans however date from before World War II, as is clear from the dull 1930s architecture. There are frequent literary and historical exhibitions, open to the public, on the ground floor. The library is one of the copyright libraries and is an important resource for scholars; admission is by ticket only. The Causewayside building (about 1.5 km to the south-east) was built, in stridently modern style, in the 1980s and 90s.

Below the Castle, building levels vary on the steep side of the hill, right down to the Grassmarket.

Central Public Library (1887 George Washington Browne): This library houses lending as well as reference departments. The Scottish Library covers all aspects of Scottish life; for information on the city, the Edinburgh Room is invaluable.

Greyfriars Kirk: It takes its name from the Franciscan friary on the site in medieval times. In 1562 Mary, Queen of Scots granted the Town Council rights to have citizens buried there, and in

1620 Greyfriars became the first new church to be built in Edinburgh after the Reformation. In 1638 the Church was the scene of one of the most important events in Scottish ecclesiastical history, when the first signatures were put to a document known as the National Covenant, which declared opposition to the episcopalian form of worship being forced on the Scottish church by Charles I.

The structure of the building has been much changed over the centuries, notably after the tower was accidentally blown up in 1718, having been used by the Town Council as a gunpowder store, and after another serious fire in 1845. In 1860 the first organ in a Scottish church since the Reformation was installed. In 1979 the congregation joined with that of Tolbooth St John's (see p.19) and services are regularly held in Gaelic as well as in English.

Greyfriars Bobby, the Skye terrier who waited 14 years by his master's grave in Greyfriars Kirkyard.

The **Kirkyard** contains monuments to many famous names in Scottish history, including George Buchanan (16th-century scholar, poet, tutor to King James VI), William Robertson (18th-century minister, historian and Principal of Edinburgh University; he was for a time minister of Greyfriars), and Duncan Ban Macintyre (18th-century Gaelic poet).

Greyfriars Bobby: The statue on the street corner outside the kirkyard commemorates the Skye terrier who remained by his master's grave for 14 years after the latter's death in 1858. The grave is to be seen just inside the entrance to Greyfriars Kirkyard and the little dog is also buried nearby.

Candlemaker Row: The old buildings on this street leading downhill to the Grassmarket include the Guildhall of the Corporation of Candlemakers (1722).

George Heriot's School (1628-60 William Wallace, William Ayton, master masons): George Heriot, the Jinglin' Geordie of Sir Walter Scott's *The Fortunes of Nigel*, was goldsmith and therefore

moneylender/banker to King James VI and his Queen, Anne of Denmark. Such were the royal finances, especially after the King's departure to London in 1603, that this was a roaring trade. He left his fortune to the city to found Heriot's Hospital for the care and education of orphan boys. The spectacular building, in the style of a Renaissance palace, is still in use as a private school (now for both sexes).

George Heriot's School, seen across the Grassmarket from Victoria Terrace.

Flodden Wall: Just to the west of the school is to be seen one of the few remaining visible sections (and the only surviving tower) of the old town wall, known as the Flodden Wall as it was built for additional defence after the battle of

1513, when King James IV was killed and his army destroyed in the north of England. The adjacent Telfer Wall dates from 1620. Another section of the Flodden Wall is visible at the bottom of the Pleasance, not far from Holyrood Palace. This wall replaced earlier medieval walls and extended protection outwards to include the Cowgate and the Grassmarket.

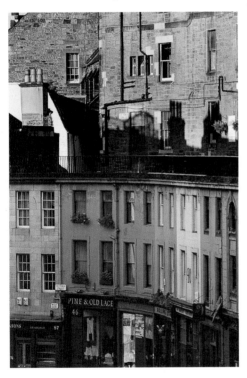

Victoria Street, an interesting haunt for eating and shopping.

Victoria Street curves downhill from the George IV Bridge towards the Grassmarket. As the name implies it was built in the 19th century, to improve access to the Old Town from the south. Above a row of pleasant restaurants and small specialist shops, **Victoria Terrace** leads through to Johnston Terrace behind the Castle.

Grassmarket: This wide street has long played a role in the city's history. Public executions took place there and in 1736 John Porteous, Captain of the City Guard, was lynched by the mob in what became known as the Porteous Riots, triggered by his vicious reaction to the disorderly crowd at the execution of a smuggler (the incident is splendidly described by Sir Walter Scott in *The Heart of Midlothian*). Today the Grassmarket is home to trendy boutiques and a variety of restaurants and pubs.

Cowgate: This street runs from the Grassmarket along the lower edge of the Old

Town. Once an upper-class suburb of the medieval city, it had become a deplorable slum by the 19th century. Today it is a busy but rather dismal thoroughfare, with one or two points of interest. **The Magdalen Chapel** was originally built as chapel to the Incorporation of Hammermen in the 1540s and the steeple was added in 1620. Much of the structure is altered but the stained glass is of interest in being the only example of pre-Reformation glass in Scotland still in its original building. It is now the headquarters of the Scottish Reformation Society, and is open to the public.

Just off the north side of the Cowgate in Niddry Street is **St Cecilia's Hall** (1763 Robert Mylne), the oldest purpose-built concert hall in Scotland, modelled on the opera house at Parma. It is also the home of the Russell Collection of early keyboard instruments. Near the eastern end of the Cowgate is **St Patrick's Church** (1772-4 John Baxter, with later alterations). Originally episcopal, it became a Catholic church in 1856.

From the Cowgate, silhouettes at dusk portray the development of the Old Town with its linking bridges.

Blackfriars Street to the north (formerly Blackfriars Wynd) takes its name from the Dominican friary founded here in the 13th century. Near the top is Regent Morton's House, a 16th-century mansion house, now used as a backpackers' hostel (see p.70).

To the south, **Robertson's Close** has an 18th-century tenement and a three-storey 17th-century house, now divided into flats.

THE NEW TOWN

By the middle of the 18th century the cramped conditions of the old Edinburgh had become a major problem and plans were made for expansion. The first growth was to the south (see George Square p.54) but by the 1760s there were

ambitious plans for development to the north, instigated partly by the influential Lord Provost of the day, George Drummond. Drainage of the Nor' Loch below the Castle Rock began in 1759, and the North Bridge, begun in 1763, was built to link the Old Town with the proposed development to the north.

In 1763 a competition for the design of the New Town was won by a young architect, James Craig, but actual building was not begun until the 1770s, with the erection of St James's Square, one building of which still survives, looking across the uncompromising

Elegant Georgian fanlights are a feature of Edinburgh's New Town doorways.

modernity of the St James shopping centre. **Princes Street**, **George Street** and **Queen Street**, with adjoining streets, formed a regular grid pattern and Craig's plan was for a square at each end, St George's (now Charlotte) Square to the west and St Andrew's (now St Andrew) Square to the east, with a church at the outer edge of each. **Charlotte Square** is indeed dominated by the green-domed St George's Church, now West Register House. The corresponding site in **St Andrew Square**, however, was bought by Sir Laurence Dundas, a wealthy local businessman and MP who already owned land just to the east of it. He built himself a fine townhouse there, now the Royal Bank of Scotland (see p.43), and St Andrew's Church (1785-7 Major Frazer), Georgian in style with a fine oval interior, was displaced to a short distance away in George Street; its congregation joined with St George's in the 1960s to form St Andrew's and St George's (see p.45).

Access from the Old Town was gradually improved with the creation of **the Mound**, a causeway built from the enormous quantities of earth and rubbish from the New Town building sites. It now curves from the middle of Princes Street up towards the High Street at Bank Street.

Further development of the New Town was slowed by the Napoleonic Wars but gradually it spread, first to the north on land largely belonging to the Heriot Trust. This area was developed in the early years of the 19th century to a design by Robert Reid and William Sibbald. To the north-east around the Calton Hill, an ambitious design by W H Playfair remained incomplete (see p.59). To the north-west from the 1820s in the estate of the Earl of Moray an elegant scheme was created (Moray Place to Randolph Crescent). For development further to the west see West End p.64.

Princes Street at dusk, dominated by the tower of the Balmoral Hotel.

Princes Street: Edinburgh's main shopping street, though it has lost most of its Georgian splendour, remains impressive in the outlook from its one side, across to the Castle, the Old Town and Princes Street Gardens. With the railway well hidden below the Castle Rock, these provide a delightful gap in the urban scene and a place for outdoor performances (when the weather permits) in the Ross Open Air Theatre. Another summer attraction for visitors is

The National Gallery of Scotland, a classical home for its international collections.

the Floral Clock, opposite the Royal Scottish Academy.

National Gallery of Scotland (1845 W H Playfair): Situated at the bottom of the Mound behind the RSA, this neo-classical building houses an exceptionally fine collection of paintings, with comprehensive Scottish collections and also examples of many ages of British and European art up to the late 19th century. (See also Scottish National Gallery of Modern Art, p.65).

Royal Scottish Academy (1832 W H Playfair): A massive neo-classical building, with some Victorian features, emphasized by a statue of that queen above the portico. As well as the

Academy's own exhibitions it houses many others, especially at Festival time.

Scott Monument (1844 G M Kemp): A soaring Victorian Gothic pile of fantastic intricacy, it could not be in greater contrast to its classical neighbours. On a clear day it affords a stunning view of the area for those energetic enough to climb its 287 steps. The Carrara marble statue of Sir Walter Scott at the base is by John Steell and the 64 niches of the monument contain statuettes representing characters from Scott's works.

Dating from the Edwardian era is the grandiose **Balmoral Hotel** (formerly the North British Hotel, 1902, W Hamilton Beattie), towering over Waverley Station, for whose former owners, the North British Railway Company, it was built, and over the Princes Mall shopping centre (on the site of the former Waverley Market).

Jenners (1893-5 J Hamilton Beattie): This opulent late-Victorian building, is still in use as an independent department store.

Register House (begun 1774 Robert Adam): Considered by many to be the finest Adam building in the city, it contains the headquarters of the National Archives of Scotland. (Part of it is now housed in West Register House, see Charlotte Square, p.44). The equestrian statue of the Duke of Wellington (1848) is by John Steell (also the sculptor of the statue of Queen Victoria above the Royal Scottish Academy as well as that of Sir Walter Scott (see above)). **New Register House** (1858-63 Robert Matheson), an Italianate building standing back from its neighbour, has the registration of births, deaths and marriages and the **Court of the Lord Lyon** (the College of Arms in Scotland).

Post Office (Robert Matheson 1861, but enlarged later): This large Italian Renaissance-style building formerly housed the main city-centre post office (now in the St James's Centre across the road). It stands on the site of the Theatre

Royal (1768), the first theatre to be built in Scotland since the Reformation. Many famous players performed there, including Mrs Sarah Siddons, whose first visit to Edinburgh in 1784 caused great excitement. The General Assembly of the Church of Scotland even rearranged its sessions so as not to clash with performances.

Café Royal (1861 Robert Paterson): A 19th-century pub and restaurant with French echoes in its style. The Circle Bar has six impressive large tile pictures of famous inventors. **The Guildford Arms** next door also dates from the 19th century (1896 R M Cameron). **The Abbotsford Bar** (1902) in Rose Street and **Milne's Bar** in Hanover Street were haunts of Edinburgh literary circles, especially in the middle of the 20th century.

Café Royal, with stained glass stressing its Victorian origins.

St Andrew Square: The eastern focus of the first New Town has seen many changes in recent years, with modern buildings and conversions of Victorian ones which had earlier replaced Georgian originals. IBM, converted **Nos. 21** and **22** in the late 1980s, retaining the original facades. No. 21 was the birthplace (in 1778) of Henry Brougham, politician and law reformer. The square is still presided over by the lofty statue (1820-3 William Burn) of Henry Dundas, First Lord Melville, who towered over Scottish and indeed British politics in the late 18th and early 19th centuries. There are also new developments in and around the bus station, see p.70.

Originally built as a grand townhouse for Sir Laurence Dundas (see p.38), the **Royal Bank of Scotland** (1772-4 Sir William Chambers) is a magnificent classical building, later home to the Excise Office (hence the royal arms above the portico) and

bought by the Royal Bank of Scotland in 1825. Many alterations were made over the years, including the addition of the splendidly domed banking hall to the rear (1857 Peddie and Kinnear). The fine equestrian statue in the forecourt (1834 Thomas Campbell) is of the fourth Earl of Hopetoun, an army commander in the Napoleonic Wars and Governor of the Bank 1820-3.

Doorways in Queen Street which has retained most of its Georgian character.

Royal College of Physicians (1844 Thomas Hamilton): The building which now houses the College at 9-10 Queen Street replaced an earlier house by a higher and grander building, with a portico not only on the doorway but also on the first-floor middle window, the latter flanked and topped by classical figures (by A H Ritchie). The adjoining No. 8 (1770-1 Robert Adam) was acquired in 1864 and the New Library (1876-7 David Bryce) was built to the rear of it; access is by arrangement. The College now also occupies No. 11, with a new conference centre to the rear.

Scottish National Portrait Gallery: Housed at the eastern end of Queen Street in a large Gothic building (1885-90 R Rowand Anderson). Built of Dumfries-shire red sandstone, it is of intricate design with numerous turrets and niches, the latter displaying figures from Scottish history. The building was formerly shared with the **Royal Museum of Scotland**, now in Chambers Street (see p.53). The Portrait Gallery, a visual history of Scotland as well as an art gallery, often houses special exhibitions and has a shop and a restaurant.

George Street: Running along the crest of the ridge, George Street has retained more of its Georgian character than Princes Street. Statues at intersections commemorate: George IV (at Hanover Street), William Pitt (at Frederick Street) and (at Castle Street) Dr Thomas Chalmers, a 19th-century Scottish churchman, who led the Disruption in 1843 (see p.10).

As well as smaller shops, George Street has numerous bank buildings, some of them now converted (into restaurants) after massive branch closure. Since 1909 it has been home to the Royal Society of Edinburgh, at Nos. 22-24 (1843 William Burn and David Bryce); the Society now embraces the humanities as well as the sciences.

Assembly Rooms (1784-7 J Henderson): The large portico was added in 1817-18 by William Burn and, along with his partner William Bryce, he added the **Music Hall** to the back in 1843. This was the centre of social life in Georgian Edinburgh; now it serves as a venue for numerous events, and is one of the liveliest centres of the Festival Fringe.

Charlotte Square: Architecturally the finest square in the city, it was originally designed, with frontages of unified style, by Robert Adam in 1791. Partly owing to the Napoleonic Wars, building was slow and only the north side was built by the end of the century; it was completed with the south side by 1820. Adam's design for St George's Church on the west side was rejected (on cost grounds) in favour of one by Robert Reid (1811); in the 1960s it was converted for use as West Register House (part of the National Archives of Scotland) and the congregation joined with St Andrew's in George Street (see p.39).

Charlotte Square has seen considerable change of ownership in recent years, with many of its financial and commercial occupiers moving out. The National Trust for Scotland has moved its headquarters from the north to the south side, and the restored centre, Nos. 26-31, incorporates also a shop, gallery, coffee house and restaurant. On the north side, its former headquarters at No. 5 is now the office of the Edinburgh World Heritage Trust. (The Old Town and the New Town together have been declared a World Heritage Site.) It was originally the town-house of a Highland laird, Grant of Rothiemurchus, whose daughter Elizabeth wrote in *Memoirs of a Highland Lady*

Charlotte Square: No.6 is now the official residence of the First Minister of the Scottish Parliament.

one of the most delightful accounts of upper-class Scottish life in the early 19th century.

No. 6, now known as **Bute House**, is used as the official residence of the First Minister of the Scottish Parliament; its third owner was Sir John Sinclair of Ulbster, landowner, agricultural improver and editor of the first *Statistical Account of Scotland (1791-8)*. The lower floors of **No. 7**, **the Georgian House**, are kept by the National Trust for Scotland as a museum of the early years of the New Town, being furnished and decorated in the style of the time.

The gardens in the centre have in recent years been the scene of the annual Edinburgh International Book Festival (see p.75), with marquees clustering round the equestrian **Albert Memorial** (1876 John Steell, see also p.41).

Heriot Row: Built in the early years of the 19th century, it continues to be one of the most elegant residential streets of the New Town, enjoying the rural view of Queen Street gardens to the south. **No. 17** was owned (1857-80) by Thomas Stevenson, one of a famous family of engineers, and was thus the childhood home of his son, Robert Louis Stevenson. The house has been maintained in mid-Victorian style.

On the northern edges of the New Town are two striking early 19th-century church buildings. The view down Frederick, Howe and St Vincent Streets is closed by the massive octagonal shape of the former **St Stephen's Church** (1827 W H Playfair), with its tall square tower and cavernous entrance. (It is now part of Stockbridge Parish Church.)

Further east, in the centre of Bellevue Crescent, **Broughton St Mary's** (1824 Thomas Brown) is in imposing Grecian style with six Corinthian columns. The tall steeple with clock tower is topped by a small dome.

HOLYROOD PARK

Holyrood Park: This wide area (over 260 ha) of open ground to the south-east of Holyrood Palace has an astonishing variety of hill, glen, loch, moor and marsh within its boundaries. The Park contains many signs of early habitation with traces of several prehistoric forts and many cultivation terraces, especially on the south-eastern slopes; some of these probably date from more recent centuries.

Arthur's Seat and Salisbury Crags loom above buildings of the Old Town.

Arthur's Seat, like the Castle Rock, part of an old volcano, gives Edinburgh the distinction of having a small mountain right at its very centre. There are many pleasant routes for walkers: some of the paths are smooth and easy enough but others are extremely rough and even precipitous; strong footwear is advised. The summit is a favourite place for viewing the city and its wider surroundings, and on a clear day it is possible to see mountains as far away as the Grampians over 160 km to the north. Though there are other theories, the name probably comes from King Arthur, prominent in the legends of the Britons who inhabited the area in the Dark Ages.

Salisbury Crags: A long steep ridge separated from the main hill by glacial action, it has further pleasant walks, with closer views of the city: a well-built path running below the upper cliffs is known as the Radical Road because its construction in 1820 provided work for some destitute radical weavers from the west of Scotland. The crest provides a brisker walk for the more adventurous. The name probably derives from the 1st Earl of Salisbury, who rested his troops near the Crags in 1337-8, or it may come from Old English meaning 'willow slope'.

Just to the east of the Radical Road is **St Margaret's Well,** a 15th-century Gothic construction which was moved in the 1860s from the village of Restalrig (now part of the city). It is fed by a natural spring.

St Anthony's Chapel: This picturesque ruin probably dates from the 15th century but little is known of its history.

There are three lochs within the Park, two of them artificial, St Margaret's Loch to the north and Dunsapie Loch to the east.

Duddingston Loch, part of the large open space of the Royal Park.

Duddingston Loch to the south is, however, natural and is a well-known bird sanctuary, with a large colony of greylag geese.

Duddingston Village: To the south-east of the Park, Duddingston retains its village character, though it is today an attractive suburb. A house in the Causeway, recently restored, has associations with Bonnie Prince Charlie, whose army had its camp at Duddingston after the Battle of Prestonpans in 1745.

Sheep's Heid Inn: Though the present building dates from about the early 19th century, the inn has been in existence since the Middle Ages; King James VI was a frequent visitor in the 16th century.

The name derives from a well-known Scottish dish of a sheep's head stewed in broth, served here into the 20th century. The inn has Scotland's oldest skittle alley.

Duddingston Kirk: Originally built in the 12th century, most of today's structure dates from the 17th and 18th, with later restoration. To the left of the kirkyard's main gate is a watchtower used to protect it from 19th-century body-snatchers. To the right of the gate is a lowpin-on-stane (mounting block) and the jougs (an iron collar used as an instrument of punishment for those who offended against church discipline).

Duddingston House (1763 William Chambers): A splendid mansion in classical style on a hill to the south-east of the village, it is now home to a firm of architects.

Prestonfield House (1687 Sir William Bruce): With its round stable block (1876), Prestonfield House can be clearly seen from Arthur's Seat across Duddingston Loch. The original house was called Priest Field, but the name was changed when it was burnt down in 1681 by a group of students opposed to the attempts of the owner, Sir James Dick, to further the Catholic cause of the Duke of York (later James VII). It was rebuilt, with its present name, to a design by Sir William Bruce (see Palace of Holyroodhouse p.31). Over the years it had many famous visitors, including Benjamin Franklin, Samuel Johnson and James Boswell. Today it is a hotel and restaurant of some distinction.

Innocent Railway: A pleasant footpath/cycleway marks the boundary of the Park along the edge of Prestonfield Golf Course. It follows the route of Edinburgh's earliest railway line, opened in 1831 to carry coal from the mines at Dalkeith, though it also became popular with passengers. The name is said to come from the fact that its trucks were originally pulled by horses, regarded as being much less dangerous than their steam successors. The line was closed in 1968.

THE UNIVERSITY & TO THE SOUTH

To the west of Holyrood Park is the main campus of the University of Edinburgh; its other main area, containing most science and engineering departments, is at King's Buildings, about 2 km to the

south. Just outside the Park are the Pollock Halls of Residence, popular as a conference centre during vacations. Their grounds are adjoined by the Royal Commonwealth Pool, built in 1967 for the 1970 Commonwealth Games; this is now Edinburgh's principal swimming pool complex (see p.76).

Scottish Widows (1972 Basil Spence, Glover and Ferguson): The modern building of Scottish Widows insurance company, of striking appearance with its hexagonal sections in dark glass, stands on the site of the printing works of Thomas Nelson, one of the many Scottish publishers who have moved to London over the years.

Queen's Hall (1823 Robert Brown): This

The Pentland Hills, to the south, above. The 19th and 20th centuries meet as the dome of the McEwan Hall (1888-97) looms behind the new Museum of Scotland (1998), left.

Georgian church was converted for use as a concert hall in 1978 (see p.74).

Archers' Hall: The home of the Royal Company of Archers, the Queen's Bodyguard in Scotland, was built in 1776-7 and extended in 1900.

Surgeons' Hall (1829-32 W H Playfair): This massively imposing neo-classical building is the home of the Royal College of Surgeons of

From the busy shopping area of Clerk Street, the Meadows stretch across to the more residential Marchmont.

Edinburgh. It has recently undergone extensive restoration. It contains exhibitions, open to the public, illustrating Edinburgh's very important role in the history of surgery; it includes a Dental Museum, and other parts of the building can be visited by arrangement.

Edinburgh Festival Theatre: For many decades the City of Edinburgh planned the creation of a new theatre spacious enough for opera, ballet and other large-scale performances at the Edinburgh International Festival. Finally in the 1990s the old Empire Theatre in Nicolson Street, recently a bingo hall, was redesigned for this purpose, with a striking glass facade. It was opened in 1994.

Chambers Street: Built in the 1860s as part of an improvement scheme, Chambers Street cleared away three old squares in its broad path. It is named after William Chambers, the Lord Provost of the time, who, with his brother Robert, founded the publishing firm of W & R Chambers (still publishing in the city, though now under French ownership). His statue surveys the scene. On the north side the former Heriot-Watt University building has been rebuilt as a new Sheriff Court House; the University has now moved to a much larger campus at Riccarton to the south-west of the city.

The south side is largely taken up by the **Royal Museum** (1860 Francis Fowke) (see also pp.44 and 74), with its lofty glass-roofed main hall. This building contains scientific collections as well as natural history, ethnography and decorative arts.

The Royal Museum of Scotland's large and impressive entrance hall in Chambers Street.

The new **Museum of Scotland,** opened in 1998, now dominates the corner of Chambers Street and George IV Bridge. On the various levels of the innovative building (Gordon Benson and Alan Forsyth, architects), it gives a vivid picture of Scotland's history and its people, as well as its geology and natural history. The museum includes educational facilities and an IT centre, and its rooftop restaurant offers one of the best panoramic views of the Old Town.

At the other end of Chambers Street is the main building of Edinburgh University, known as the **Old College,** or more familiarly as the Old Quad, fronting onto the South Bridge. Robert Adam's design of 1789 was completed in 1818-34 by William Playfair, who designed most of the interiors, including the magnificent **Playfair Library**, now used for ceremonial purposes only, since the opening of the new Library in George Square in 1965. The east bay houses the **Talbot Rice Art Gallery** (see p.74). The dome, an enlarged version of Adam's design, is by R Rowand Anderson (1879). He was also responsible for the **McEwan Hall** (1888-97), the University's graduation hall, and the adjoining Medical School (1876-86), together forming a complex in opulent Venetian Renaissance style.

George Square: One of the early jewels of Georgian architecture in Edinburgh, it was largely destroyed by University planning in the 1960s. Only the west side survives intact, along with a few houses on the east; these still house several University departments. The David Hume and Appleton Towers do much to ruin Edinburgh's otherwise relatively unspoilt skyline on the east side, though the other modern university buildings are less offensive.

Meadows: Before being drained in the 17th–19th centuries, the tree-lined open space between the University/Royal Infirmary and the Marchmont area of the city was the South, or Burgh Loch. Today it provides a pleasant place for many kinds of recreation, from lunch-time strolls to the annual Meadows Festival in June.

The area is due to change in the early years of the century with the move of the Royal Infirmary to Little France on the south-east edge of the city. The late 19th-century buildings are to be redeveloped with their prime site.

Bruntsfield Links: To the south-west another

open space had long associations with the game of golf, continued at the present time only in a short-hole course. The **Golf Tavern** on the west side stands on the site of an 18th-century inn which was home to several early golfing societies.

South of these open spaces are some of Edinburgh's most popular suburbs. To the south-east are the elegant villas of the Grange, to the

south, Marchmont and Bruntsfield with their forest of Victorian and Edwardian tenement flats, a form of dwelling which is more European than British.

To the south-west Morningside stretches out towards the hills in rows of terraces and villas, creating a comfortingly genteel atmosphere, so that 'Morningside' has often been used to describe a unique style of Edinburgh accent. Today's inhabitants are of mixed origins and all kinds of voices will be heard, from broad Edinburgh Scots to southern English.

The Royal Infirmary and University spires above the trees of the Meadows.

STOCKBRIDGE & TO THE NORTH

The Stockbridge area, to the north-west of the New Town, was developed from 1813 onwards by Henry Raeburn, one of Scotland's greatest portrait painters, and his name is still recalled in its main street, **Raeburn Place**, now a popular shopping

Alternating doors and stairs of the Stockbridge Colonies.

area for those who prefer smaller traditional shops to massive shopping centres. His wife is remembered in **Ann Street**, one of Edinburgh's most elegant residential streets.

To the north are the **Stockbridge Colonies**, an interesting development of the 1860s to provide good housing for working people. The 11 rows of two-storey terrace houses have lower flats entered from one side and upper from the other, in the adjoining street, via an outside stair.

A short distance west of Raeburn Place, on the north side of Comely Bank Road, Comely Bank is an elegant Georgian terrace amid largely Victorian surroundings. **No. 21** was the home of Thomas and Jane Welsh Carlyle from 1826-8.

Fettes College (1862-70 David Bryce): An imposing building on an equally imposing site, it combines French château style with Scottish baronial. Founded as an independent school for boys, in recent years it has had girl pupils also. Another striking school building, **Daniel Stewart's & Melville College**, stands above the Queensferry

Road. Formerly Daniel Stewart's College (1848 David Rhind), it is in florid Jacobean style.

Inverleith Park stretches east from Fettes, extending the open space provided by the **Royal Botanic Garden**. Justly famous as a showplace as well as a research institute, the Garden, which has been on its present site since 1824, has its origin in the late 17th-century Physic Gardens, where medicinal plants were grown. (An early garden was sited where Waverley Station now stands.)

The octagonal Old Palm House (1834) contrasts with the New Glass Houses of the 1960s. They give not only much of botanical (and zoological) interest, but on occasion a welcome

Fettes College from the Queensferry Road – a striking building in a striking position.

shelter from the rigours of the Edinburgh climate. Colour in the Garden reaches a peak in April-May with the brilliant flowering of rhododendrons and azaleas.

The rock garden to the south has year-round colour, and its apex has one of the Garden's finest

The Royal Botanic Garden, with the pleasure both of its plants, and of views towards the city centre and castle.

panoramic views of the city skyline. The other is higher up in front of **Inverleith House**, a rather severe Georgian mansion, used from 1960-84 as the Scottish National Gallery of Modern Art (see p.65) and still used for occasional exhibitions. An adjoining tearoom shares the panoramic view.

On the hillside below is the recently constructed Chinese garden, with its collection of Chinese plants, many of them surprisingly familiar in a Scottish garden. Landscaping with cascading streams adds to the atmosphere.

Canonmills, the district near the east gate of the Garden, takes its name from the mills built here by the canons of Holyrood on land granted to them by King David I in the 12th century.

Robert Louis Stevenson is remembered at three points in the area: his birthplace at 8 Howard Place, the little school he attended in Rodney Street (now a Baptist Church), and another childhood home at 1 Inverleith Terrace (now No. 9) where he lived till age six (see also p.46).

CALTON HILL & TO THE EAST

Above the east end of Princes Street, **Calton Hill** intensifies Edinburgh's 'Athens of the North' image, especially with the massive pillars of the **National Monument.** It was intended to be a replica of the Parthenon, as a memorial to the

dead of the Napoleonic Wars; the west side was built in the 1820s (C R Cockerell, W H Playfair), but funds could not be raised for its completion. To the south-west the **Nelson Monument** (1807 Robert Burn), in the shape of an upturned telescope, towers even higher, providing an excellent viewpoint on a clear day. A large ball on the flagpole is raised and dropped at 1pm as a time signal. To the north is the **City Observatory** (1818 W H Playfair) in domed Grecian style; in 1895 the Observatory had to move to the cleaner air of Blackford Hill on the south side of the city. The Astronomical Society of Edinburgh open it to the public on Friday evenings. The adjacent **Observatory House** with

Calton Hill and its many monuments, looking towards the Firth of Forth.

its Gothic towers is of earlier date and was designed by James Craig, architect of the first New Town (see p.38). On the south-east is a monument to Professor John Playfair, mathematician, physicist and geologist, designed by his nephew, W H Playfair.

The monument just below (1831 W H Playfair) to Dugald Stewart, philosopher of the Scottish Enlightenment, is echoed in its Greek-temple style by

The city centre from Calton Hill in the last light of a warm summer evening.

the **Burns Monument** (1830 Thomas Hamilton) on the other side of Regent Road. Its striking design and prominent position are a fitting tribute to Scotland's greatest poet. It overlooks the **New Calton Burial Ground,** opened in 1821. The circular watchtower reminds of the danger of grave-robbers at that time. It replaced part of **Old Calton Burial Ground**, closer to Princes Street, which disappeared in the creation of Waterloo Place; the surviving section contains many interesting old gravestones and monuments, notably one to David Hume, the Enlightenment philosopher. The tall obelisk at the centre (1844 Thomas Hamilton) is to the memory of Thomas Muir and other political martyrs of the 1790s. **The Emancipation**

Monument (1893 George E Bissell), with its statue of Abraham Lincoln, commemorates Scottish-American soldiers who took part in the American Civil War.

New Parliament House (1825-9 Thomas Hamilton) – formerly the old Royal High School: This Greek Doric building on a striking site below the Calton Hill replaced the 18th-century Royal High School in Infirmary Street on the south side of the city. The school's origins go back to the 12th century when it was associated with Holyrood Abbey. From the 15th century it was run by the Town Council. The school moved once more in the 1960s, to Barnton, in the northwest, and in the late 1970s this building was altered for the proposed Scottish Assembly. In the 1990s, as devolution became more likely, it became known as New Parliament House.

The Nelson Monument on Calton Hill dominates the rather heavy facade of St Andrew's House.

St Andrew's House (1936-9 Thomas S Tait): Built for the Scottish Office (now the Scottish Executive), it massively proclaims its governmental purpose and its 1930s origin. It was built on the site of the Calton Jail, once Scotland's largest prison, replacing the Old Tolbooth in the High Street (see p.23). All that remains of the jail is the **Governor's House**, with its towers and battlements on a precipitous site above Waverley Station.

New St Andrew's House: Former home of the Scottish Office, most of which moved to Leith in the 1990s, and the St James's shopping centre (1964-70) form an undistinguished cluster of buildings, slightly improved in recent years by an extension to the John Lewis store in Leith Street. They replaced the elegant simplicity of St James's Square, one section of which can still be seen.

Picardy Place: A pleasant open traffic node to the north-west of the Calton Hill, still retaining some Georgian buildings, dating from the early 1800s. It was built on the site of a weavers' village set up in the early 18th century for a colony of Huguenot silk-weavers, escaping from religious persecution in France; hence the name. Sir Arthur Conan Doyle was born at No. 11 in 1859 and is commemorated here by a plaque opposite his (now demolished) birthplace, and by a statue of Sherlock Holmes (1991 Gerald Laing) on the north side.

St Mary's Metropolitan Cathedral (Roman Catholic): Only the facade remains of the Catholic chapel (1813 James Gillespie Graham) built when the Catholic church was once more able to worship openly. Many alterations were made over the years and it became a cathedral in 1878. On the widened pavement outside are three statues, including a giant hand and foot (1990 Eduardo Paolozzi).

Playhouse Theatre (1927-9 J Fairweather): Originally Edinburgh's largest cinema, with seating for over 3000, it was recently renovated and is now used mainly as a theatre.

To the north of the Calton Hill is the last major development of the New Town, based on an ambitious design of 1819 by W H Playfair. It was only partially completed, and that over many years. It includes the rather grand terraces curving round the hill, **Regent Terrace** to the south, **Carlton Terrace** round the eastern end and **Royal Terrace** to the north. Some further terraces were eventually built across London Road, the main thoroughfare to the east.

Meadowbank Sports Centre (see p.75) was built for the Commonwealth Games in 1970. Nearby is the **Easter Road** ground of one of the city's two main football teams, Hibernian, with a new stadium built in the 1990s.

The long wide street running north-east is Leith Walk, leading into **Leith**, Edinburgh's port and until 1920 a separate burgh outside the city boundary. It still maintains much of the individual character of an independent town and many old buildings, some dating back to medieval times, remind of the days when it was engaged in trade with Europe. In particular the wine trade was strong and claret imported from France was a national drink long before whisky.

There has been much restoration and building, including a new office block for the Scottish Executive (formerly the Scottish Office), opened in 1995 at Victoria Quay. Restaurants have sprung up along the waterfront, many of them specializing in seafood, especially on the Shore, a quayside street where the Water of Leith meets the harbour. The Royal Yacht *Britannia*, now berthed at Leith, has become a popular tourist attraction; buses run from the Waverley Bridge in the city centre.

Leith, Edinburgh's port, and one of its waterfronts.

THE WEST END & TO THE WEST

On the west side of the city are two of its main sporting venues. At **Tynecastle**, off Gorgie Road, is the ground for one of Edinburgh's two main football teams, Heart of Midlothian (see also p.25). Not far away is **Murrayfield Rugby**

The Scottish National Gallery of Modern Art, one of Edinburgh's classical buildings.

Ground, scene of many famous matches, the fans of both participating sides filling Edinburgh with jollification before and after.

Corstorphine Hill to the north-west is a long wooded ridge, now a public park, and at its southern end is **Edinburgh Zoo**. Run by the Royal Zoological Society of Scotland, the Zoo covers 80 acres of the hillside and has a worldwide reputation for conservation. It boasts the world's biggest penguin house.

Closer to the centre a large striking building in Jacobean style is seen on the north side of the Glasgow Road, **Donaldson's School for the Deaf** (1842-54 W H Playfair). It was founded as an orphanage on an endowment left by James Donaldson, an Edinburgh printer and newspaper proprietor.

Haymarket Station (1840): With its two-storey building in classical style, Haymarket is said to be the oldest station in Scotland still in use in its original form. It was the original terminus of the Glasgow-Edinburgh railway.

Also to the west of centre is the **Scottish National Gallery of Modern Art** (see p.74). A building in Greek Doric style (1825 William Burn), it was formerly John Watson's School. The collection contains Scottish and international art of the 20th century (see also National Gallery of Scotland p.40).The surrounding park provides an outdoor setting for sculptures and other outdoor works of art (and for lunch if the Edinburgh climate permits!) It is now possible to approach the Gallery on foot from the Water of Leith Walkway behind (see p.77).

Dean Gallery (1831-3 Thomas Hamilton): Formerly the Orphan Hospital, later an education centre, it has recently become one of the National Galleries of Scotland, housing sculpture and drawings by Eduardo Paolozzi (gifted by the artist), and Dada and Surrealist collections.

Dean Village from Belford Road.

Further along the Water of Leith is the **Dean Village**, nestling on the riverbank below the majestic span of Thomas Telford's **Dean Bridge** (1829-31). Formerly called the Water of Leith Village, it grew around the flour mills which had used the river's water power for centuries. It is now a popular residential area with houses which are mostly more picturesque than spacious. Some of the old mill buildings have been converted into flats, while others are used for commercial purposes. There are also new residential developments.

West End: The mainly residential area to the south-west of the first New Town consists of Georgian and Victorian terraces and crescents of opulent proportions. The skyline is dominated by the three Gothic spires of **St Mary's Cathedral** (1874-1917 Sir George Gilbert Scott), the cathedral for the episcopal diocese of Edinburgh. **St Mary's Music School**, now housed in Coates Hall, a Robert Lorimer building nearby, provides specialist musical and general education for the Cathedral choristers and for gifted young musicians from all parts of Scotland and elsewhere.

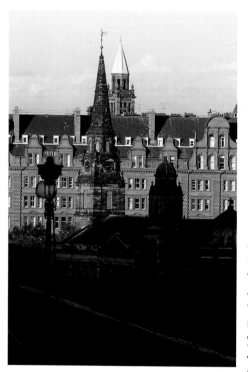

The Caledonian Hotel with West End church towers.

St George's West Church (1866-9 David Bryce): Its Italian style is further accentuated, though in a different way, by the later addition of a campanile (1879 R Rowand Anderson), based on that of S. Giorgio Maggiore in Venice.

Caledonian Hotel (1899-1903 J M Dick Peddie and G Washington Browne): This large ornate red sandstone building was built at the terminus of the Caledonian Railway at Princes Street Station and indeed incorporates three arches built earlier as a station entrance.

King's Theatre (1905-6 J D Swanston): This Edwardian theatre at Tollcross is one of Edinburgh's main theatrical venues (see p.74).

Royal Lyceum Theatre (1883 C J Phipps): Classical in style with an opulent (and recently renovated) interior, this is the city's main drama theatre and it is host to many important Festival productions (see p.74). Next to it is the **Usher Hall** (1910-14 J Stockdale Harrison): endowed by the brewer Andrew Usher, this is Edinburgh's largest concert hall with seating for 2900. Its octagonal shape with green dome is conspicuous in the area below the Castle (see p.75).

It is adjoined by **Saltire Court** (1991 Campbell and Arnott), a large office block which occupies a long-vacant site which became known as 'the hole in the ground'! It also houses the **Traverse Theatre.** Opened in the 1960s as an experimental theatre in tiny premises in the Lawnmarket, the Traverse moved to the West Bow close by in 1969. In 1992 it moved to this modern home below Saltire Court, but the policy of producing new plays by modern, especially Scottish, authors continues (see p.74).

The 19th-century buildings of the area have recently been overshadowed by modern development. The **Sheraton Hotel** (1982 Crerar and Partners) rises massively behind the new Festival Square, but has itself been overtaken by larger and more modern office buildings, including new headquarters for Scottish Widows and Standard Life, in an area known as the **Exchange**.

The Edinburgh International Conference Centre (1994 Terry Farrell): Opened in 1995, this striking modern building aims to attract prestigious conferences to the city.

St John's Church (1815-18 William Burn): This episcopal church, at the corner of Princes Street and Lothian Road, is an early example of the Gothic Revival and has a fine interior. It has a café and shops in the restored undercroft, and is much involved in publicizing and dealing with Third World issues.

St Cuthbert's Parish Church (1892-5 Hippolyte J Blanc): Since medieval times, there has been a church on this site below the Castle dedicated to St Cuthbert, the Northumbrian shepherd boy who became Bishop of Lindisfarne and is Edinburgh's patron saint. It was originally

The Castle stands out against the back-drop of Arthur's Seat, seen from the west, above.

outside the city and served as a parish church for the surrounding countryside. The present Renaissance-style building retains the steeple of its 18th-century predecessor. It is situated well below Princes Street and is best viewed, along with its large churchyard, from Princes Street Gardens. The two-storey crenellated **Watch House** (1827) dates back to the time of the infamous Burke and Hare grave-robberies.

Edinburgh Castle and the city from Salisbury Crags at dusk, opposite.

INFORMATION DIRECTORY

PLEASE NOTE: When telephoning from Edinburgh, omit 0131 from all numbers. Addresses are all Edinburgh unless stated otherwise.

Information Centre
3 Princes St, EH2
tel: 0131 473 3800
email: esic@eltb.org
www.edinburgh.org

Tourist Information Desk
Edinburgh Airport Main Concourse
tel: 0131 333 1000

ACCOMMODATION

Information and reservations for **Hotels** and **Guest Houses** can be obtained from the Information Centre (see above)

Youth Hostels
Backpackers Hostel,
65 Cockburn Street, EH1
tel: 0131 220 1717
email: info@hoppo.com

Bruntsfield Youth Hostel,
7 Bruntsfield Cresc, EH10
tel: 0131 447 2994

Eglinton Youth Hostel,
18 Eglinton Cresc, EH12
tel: 0131 337 1120

High Street Hostel,
8 Blackfriars St, EH1
tel: 0131 557 3984
email: high-street@scotlands-top-hostels.com

Caravan and Camping Sites
Drummohr Caravan Park, Levenhall,
Musselburgh, EH21
tel: 0131 665 6867

Mortonhall Caravan Park,
Frogston Rd East, EH16
tel: 0131 664 1533

Edinburgh Caravan Club Site,
Marine Drive, EH4
tel: 0131 312 6874

TRAVEL

Air
Edinburgh Airport
tel: 0131 333 1000
There are regular bus services to the airport from Waverley Bridge.

Rail
Edinburgh Waverley Station,
Waverley Bridge
tel: 08457 484950

Bus
Traveline,
2 Cockburn Street
tel: 0131 225 3858;
local calls 0800 232323
Traveline has information on all local public transport services, especially buses. They produce a free map of the routes and times of all the major bus companies.

St Andrew Square Bus Station
Edinburgh's bus station is being rebuilt and is due for completion in 2002. It will be adjoined to a new shopping centre, to include a Harvey Nichols store. Meanwhile buses arrive and depart at various points in St Andrew Square and nearby streets, and notices indicate departure points for various directions.

City Tours
Lothian Region Transport (0131 555 6363) and Guide Friday (0131 556 2244), both run fleets of open-topped buses, with regular historical tours of the city from the Waverley Bridge.

Taxi
Taxis in the city are usually plentiful and the majority will take wheelchairs. They can be hailed in the street, picked up at various ranks or phoned. Listed below are the phone numbers of some of the most widely used companies:

Capital Castle Taxis
tel: 0131 228 2555

Central Radio Taxis
tel: 0131 229 2468

City Cabs
tel: 0131 228 1211

Edinburgh Airport Taxi Association
tel: 0131 334 3344

Radiocabs
tel: 0131 225 9000

POLICE

Lothian and Borders Police HQ,
Fettes Ave, EH4
tel: 0131 311 3131

LOST PROPERTY

Police (as above)
tel: 0131 311 3141

Waverley Station
tel: 0131 556 2477

Lothian Buses
tel: 0131 558 8858

BANKS/BUREAUX DE CHANGE (outside bank hours)

Banks
Most of the banks in the city provide exchange facilities. Normal banking hours are 9.30–16.30.

Bureaux de Change
Information Centre,
3 Princes St, EH2
tel: 0131 557 3953

Waverley Station
tel: 0131 557 2784

Edinburgh Airport
tel: 0131 333 3146

American Express
16 Hanover St, EH2
tel: 0131 220 0077
139 Princes St, EH2
tel: 0131 718 2501

Thomas Cook
52 Hanover St, EH2
tel:0131 226 5500
28 Frederick St
tel: 0131 465 7700

CONSULATES

American,
3 Regent Ter, EH7
tel: 0131 556 8315

Australian,
Hobart House, 80 Hanover St, EH2
tel: 0131 226 6271

Belgian,
2 West St, Penicuik
tel: 01968 679970

Chinese,
Romano House
43 Station Road, EH12
tel: 0131 334 8501

Dutch,
113 Dundas St, EH3
tel: 0131 550 5000

French,
11 Randolph Cres, EH3
tel: 0131 225 7954

German,
16 Eglinton Cres, EH12
tel: 0131 337 2323

Greek,
16 Gordon Ter, EH3
tel: 0131 667 3036

Irish,
16 Randolph Cres, EH3
tel: 0131 226 7711

Italian,
32 Melville St, EH3
tel: 0131 226 3631

Japanese,
2 Melville Cres, EH3
tel: 0131 225 4777

Monaco,
39 Castle St, EH2
tel: 0131 225 1200

Norwegian,
86 George St, EH2
tel: 0131 226 5701

Philippines,
1/3 Bankhead Medway
tel: 453 3222

Polish,
2 Kinnear Rd, EH3
tel: 0131 552 0301

Russian Federation,
58 Melville St, EH3
tel: 0131 225 7098

Spanish,
63 North Castle St, EH2
tel: 0131 220 1843

Swedish,
22 Hanover St
tel: 0131 229 6050

MEDICAL SERVICES

For an ordinary illness or a minor
accident, your hotel or place of
residence can usually put you in
touch with a local doctor or dentist.
For emergencies:
Dial 999
(for fire, police or ambulance).

Royal Infirmary of Edinburgh,
Lauriston Pl, EH3
tel: 0131 536 1000

For dental emergencies out of hours,
contact
Western General Hospital,
Crewe Road South
tel: 0131 537 1000

Late-opening chemist:
Boots,
48 Shandwick Place EH2
tel: 0131 225 6757

PLACES OF WORSHIP

Church of Scotland
St Giles Cathedral,
High St, EH1
tel: 0131 225 4363 (see p.22)
.
Greyfriars Tolbooth and
Highland Kirk, Greyfriars Pl, EH1
tel: 0131 225 1900;
also has services in Gaelic (see p.33)

St Andrew's and St George's,
George St, EH2
tel: 0131 225 3847 (see p.39)

Scottish Episcopal
St Mary's Cathedral,
Palmerston Pl, EH12
tel: 0131 225 2978 (see p.66)

St John's,
Princes St, EH2
tel: 0131 229 7565 (see p.67)

Roman Catholic
St Mary's Metropolitan Cathedral,
Broughton St
tel: 0131 556 1798 (see p.62)

St Patrick's Church,
Cowgate
tel: 0131 556 1973 (see p.37)

Methodist
Central Hall,
2 West Tollcross
tel: 0131 221 9029

Baptist
Charlotte Chapel,
West Rose St

Free Church of Scotland
Buccleuch and Greyfriars,
West Crosscauseway & Buccleuch St
tel: 0131 667 4651

Salvation Army
East Adam St
1 East Adam St
tel: 0131 669 8257

Orthodox
Orthodox Community and
Chaplaincy of St Andrew
23a George Sq, EH8
tel: 0131 667 0372

Quaker
Society of Friends Quaker Meeting
House, 7 Victoria Terr, EH1
tel: 0131 225 4825

Jewish
Edinburgh Hebrew Congregation,
4 Salisbury Rd, EH16
tel: 0131 667 3144

Islamic
Central Mosque,
50 Potterrow, EH8
tel: 0131 667 0140

Pakistan Association Mosque Centre,
11 Pilrig St, EH6
tel: 0131 554 9904

MUSEUMS, ART GALLERIES, EXHIBITIONS

Brass-rubbing Centre,
High St, EH1
tel: 0131 556 4364 (see p.27)

Camera Obscura,
Outlook Tower,
Castlehill, EH1
tel: 0131 226 3709 (see p.19)

City Art Centre,
Market St, EH1
tel: 0131 529 3993

Dean Gallery,
Belford Road, EH4
tel: 0131 624 6200 (see p.65)

Fruitmarket Gallery,
45 Market St, EH1
tel: 0131 225 2383

Huntly House Museum,
Canongate, EH8
Tel: 0131 529 4143 (see p.28)

John Knox House,
43 High St, EH1 1SR
tel: 0131 556 9579/2647 (see p.26)

Lauriston Castle,
Cramond Road South, EH4
tel: 0131 336 2060

Museum of Childhood,
42 High St, EH1
tel: 0131 529 4142 (see p.26)

Museum of Scotland,
Chambers Street, EH1
tel: 0131 247 4422
web: www.nms.ac.uk (see p.53)

National Archives of Scotland,
H M General Register House
tel: 0131 535 1360 (see p.41)

National Gallery of Scotland,
The Mound, EH2
tel: 0131 624 6200
recorded information:
0131 332 2266
web: natgalscot.ac.uk (see p.40)

National Library of Scotland,
George IV Bridge, EH1
tel: 0131 226 4531 (see p.33)

National War Museum of Scotland,
The Castle, EH1
tel: 0131 225 7534 (see p.15)

Nelson Monument,
Calton Hill, EH7 (see p.59)

Netherbow Arts Centre,
see John Knox House p.27

Newhaven Heritage Museum,
Pier Place
Newhaven Harbour
tel: 0131 551 4165

People's Story Museum,
Canongate Tolbooth
Canongate, EH8
tel: 0131 225 2424 (see p.28)

Royal Museum
Chambers St, EH1
tel: 0131 225 7534 (see p.53)

Royal Observatory,
Blackford Hill
tel: 0131 668 8405
Visitor Centre open all year

Royal Scottish Academy,
The Mound, EH2
tel: 0131 225 6671 (see p.40)

Scott Monument,
Princes St, EH2
tel: 0131 529 4068 (see p.41)

Scottish National Gallery of
Modern Art, Belford Rd, EH4
tel: 0131 624 6200 (see p.65)

Scottish National Portrait Gallery,
1 Queen St, EH2
tel: 0131 624 6200 (see p.44)

Stills Gallery,
23 Cockburn St. EH1
tel: 0131 622 6200

Talbot Rice Art Gallery,
South Bridge, EH8
tel: 0131 650 2210 (see p.54)

Writers' Museum
(formerly Lady Stair's House),
Lawnmarket, EH1
tel: 0131 529 4901 (see p.21)

LIBRARIES

Central Public Library,
George IV Bridge, EH1
Tel: 0131 242 8000; will provide
information on branches throughout
the city (see p.33)

National Library of Scotland,
George IV Bridge, EH1
Tel: 0131 226 4531; has exhibitions
open to the public (see p.33)

THEATRES, CONCERT HALLS
(box office numbers)

Assembly Rooms,
George St, EH2
tel: 0131 220 4349

Bedlam Theatre,
2 Forrest Road, EH3
tel: 0131 225 9873

Church Hill Theatre,
Morningside Road, EH10
tel: 0131 447 7597

Edinburgh Festival Theatre,
13–29 Nicolson St EH8
tel: 0131 529 6000

King's Theatre,
Leven Street, EH3
tel: 0131 529 6000

Netherbow Arts Centre,
43-45 High St, EH1
tel: 0131 556 9579

Playhouse Theatre,
18-22 Greenside Pl, EH1
tel: 0870 606 3424

Queen's Hall,
37 Clerk St, EH8
tel: 0131 668 2019

Ross Open Air Theatre,
Princes St Gardens
tel: 0131 228 8616

Royal Lyceum Theatre,
Grindlay St, EH3
tel: 0131 248 4848

St Cecilia's Hall
Niddrie St, EH1
tel: 0131 650 2423

Theatre Workshop,
34 Hamilton Pl, EH3
tel: 0131 226 5425

Traverse Theatre,
Cambridge St, EH1
tel: 0131 228 1404

Usher Hall,
Lothian Rd, EH1
tel: 0131 228 8616

CINEMAS
(box office numbers)

ABC,
120 Lothian Rd, EH3
tel: 0131 229 3030

Cameo Cinema,
38 Home St, EH3
tel: 0131 228 4141

Dominion Cinema,
Newbattle Terr, EH10
tel: 0131 447 2660

Filmhouse,
88 Lothian Rd, EH3
tel: 0131 228 2668
Odeon,
7 Clerk St, EH8
tel: 0131 667 0971

UCG,
Fountain Park
Dundee Street, EH11
tel: 0870 902 0417

UCI Cinemas,
7 Kinnaird Park,
Newcraighall Rd, EH15
tel: 0131 669 0777

FESTIVAL INFORMATION

Edinburgh Festival Fringe,
180 High St, EH1
tel: 0131 226 5257

Edinburgh Folk Festival,
Greenside Pl, EH1
tel: 0131 556 3181

Edinburgh International Book Festival,
137 Dundee St, EH11
tel: 0131 228 5444

Edinburgh International Festival,
The Hub, Castlehill, EH1
tel: 0131 473 2000
email: thehub@eif.co.uk
www.eif.co.uk

Edinburgh International Film Festival,
88 Lothian Road, EH3
tel: 0131 229 2550
email: info@edfilmfest.org.uk

Edinburgh International Jazz Festival,
29 St Stephen St, EH3
tel: 0131 225 2202

Edinburgh International Science
Festival
8 Lochend Road, EH6
tel: 0131 530 2001
email: esf@scifest.demon.co.uk
www.eif.co.uk

Edinburgh Military Tattoo,
22 Market St, EH1
Tel: 0131 225 1188
email: edintattoo@edintattoo.co.uk

SPORTS AND LEISURE
CENTRES (indoor)

For further information on sport and
outdoor activities,
tel: 0131 317 1991

Ainslie Park,
92 Pilton Dr, EH5
tel: 0131 551 2400

Craiglockhart,
177 Colinton Rd, EH14
tel: 0131 443 0101

Gracemount,
22 Gracemount Dr, EH16
tel: 0131 658 1940

Jack Kane Centre,
208 Niddrie Mains Rd, EH16
tel: 0131 669 0404

Meadowbank,
139 London Rd, EH7
tel: 0131 661 5351

Saughton Sports Complex,
Stevenson Dr, EH11
tel: 0131 444 0422

Wester Hailes Education Centre,
Murrayburn Dr, EH14
tel: 0131 442 2201

Swimming Pools
Royal Commonwealth Pool,
Dalkeith Rd, EH16
tel: 0131 667 7211 for opening
times and information on all
Edinburgh swimming pools

Dalry,
Caledonian Cresc, EH11

Glenogle,
22 Glenogle Rd, EH3

Leith Victoria,
Junction Place, EH6

Leith Waterworld,
377 Easter Road, EH6

Portobello,
Promenade, EH15

Warrender Swim Centre,
Thirlestane Rd, EH9

Golf Courses (public)
Braid Hills,
Braid Hills Road, EH10
tel: 0131 447 6666

Carrick Knowe,
Balgreen Road, EH12
tel: 0131 337 1096

Craigentinny,
Craigentinny Ave, EH7
tel: 0131 554 7501

Portobello,
Stanley St, EH15
tel: 0131 669 4361

Silverknowes,
Silverknowes Parkway, EH4
tel: 0131 336 3843

Bowling Greens (public)
Balgreen
Balgreen Rd

East Meadows

Leith Links

Powderhall
Broughton Road

St Margaret's Park,
Corstorphine
High St

Victoria Park,
Newhaven Road

Ten-Pin Bowling
Marco's Eurobowl,
146 Slateford Road, EH14
tel: 0131 443 2211

Megabowl,
Kinnaird Park
New Craighall Road
tel: 0131 657 3731

Ice Rink
Murrayfield Ice Rink,
Riversdale Cres
tel: 0131 337 6933

Artificial Ski Slope
Midlothian Ski Centre,
Hillend
Biggar Rd
tel: 0131 445 4433

SHOPPING

Princes Street is still Edinburgh's main
shopping street (see p.39) and has
several standard High-Street stores
such as Marks & Spencer, BHS, Boots,
a few remaining department stores,
including the independent Jenners
(see p.41), and numerous small
shops, many of them catering for
tourists. The parallel Rose Street and
George Street have mainly smaller
shops, the former with pedestrian
precinct.

At the eastern end of Princes Street
are two modern shopping centres,
the St James centre with John Lewis
Partnership and many smaller establishments, and the Princes Mall shopping centre, on the site of the old
Waverley Market above the Station.
It consists of small specialist shops
and has a large foodcourt on the

ground floor. Cameron Toll shopping centre on the south-east of the city is popular for car-shopping. But Edinburgh's largest is the Gyle shopping centre, on the west side of the city, off the Glasgow Road, near its junction with the City Bypass; Safeway and Marks & Spencer flank numerous smaller shops and services.

WALKS

Walking tours are very popular and are organized by several groups. Information can be found at the Tourist Information Centre and the groups often advertise by placard at their starting points, for example in the High Street. They include ghost tours along the Royal Mile, some of them held at night (though the hours of darkness are few in midsummer!)

The city is fortunate in having country walks starting at its very centre; the following are one or two suggestions:

1. Arthur's Seat (see also p.47) This is just one suggestion; there are endless variations:

Start at the carpark behind Holyrood Palace, cross the road and take the steep ascending path to the right, below the cliffs of the Salisbury Crags. At the top, turn left and cross to the foot of Arthur's Seat; turn left again along a bushy path. Turn right up some steep steps leading to an open space. From there a steep winding path leads to the summit. Descend by this path and then straight back down, turning left at the bottom to reach the carpark.

2. Royal Botanic Garden (see p.57) Start from either gate: the East Gate in Inverleith Row is accessible to bus routes; the West Gate in Arboretum Road is more convenient for parking. From the west side, your walk can be extended into Inverleith Park and both gates are close to the Water of Leith Walkway (see below).

3. The Water of Leith Walkway stretches from Balerno, on the south-west edge of the city to the port of Leith. It now has a visitor centre in an old school building just off the Lanark road. Near the city centre you can pick it up below the Scottish National Gallery of Modern Art in Belford Road and follow it, with interruptions via streets, through the Dean Village and thence to Stockbridge. It skirts the Botanic Garden and, after a section along an old railway (approached from Warriston Crescent), it winds its way down to Leith, ending up at the Shore, where the thirsty walker will find a good variety of pubs and restaurants.

CYCLE WAYS

There is a good range of cycle paths throughout Edinburgh, more information can be obtained from:
Traveline
2 Cockburn St.

SPOKES, a local pressure group, publishes a citywide map of cycleways, available in cycle shops and book shops.

DISTILLERIES

The Scotch Whisky Association produces a list of distilleries throughout Scotland which welcome visitors; the nearest to Edinburgh is Glenkinchie, near Pencaitland, about 19 km to the east. The list and further information can be had from:
Scotch Whisky Heritage Centre, The Royal Mile
354 Castlehill, EH2
Tel: 0131 220 0441 (see also p.18)

ACTIVITIES FOR CHILDREN

To find places of interest for children of all ages see also sports centres and swimming pools.

Brass-rubbing centre
(see pp.23 and 73)

Camera Obscura
(see pp.19 and 73)

Deep Sea World
North Queensferry
Fife
tel: 0906 941 0077
A gigantic aquarium with a moving
walkway along the sea bed.

Dynamic Earth, Holyrood Road, EH8
tel: 0131 550 7800 (see p.32)

Edinburgh Butterfly and Insect World
Dobbie's Garden World, Lasswade
EH18
tel: 0131 663 4932
email: ebiw@compuserve.com

Edinburgh Zoo
Corstorphine Road, EH12
tel: 0131 334 9171
(see p.64)

Gorgie Farm Project
Gorgie Rd, EH11
tel: 0131 337 4202

Museum of Childhood
(see pp.22 and 73)

Nelson Monument
Calton Hill
(see p.59)

Royal Museum
Chambers St
(see p.74)

Royal Botanic Garden
Inverleith Row, EH3
tel: 0131 552 7171
(see p.56)

Royal Observatory
Blackford Hill, EH9
tel: 0131 668 8405

Scott Monument
(see pp.38 and 74)

RESTAURANTS

Edinburgh has a wealth of restaurants, with opportunities to sample cuisine from all corners of the globe, including Thai, Nepalese and Mexican cooking. The large hotels tend towards the usual international approach but some do try to offer the best in Scottish cooking. 'A Taste of Scotland' publishes a book listing hotels and restaurants in their scheme. There are good restaurants throughout the city but certain areas have a greater concentration. Hanover Street has food from all over the world, the Nicholson Square area, catering for students, has many at the cheaper end of the market. Lothian Road and Queensferry St at the West End have numerous restaurants, including several Italian. Leith has many excellent restaurants, some of them specializing in seafood, as one might expect from Edinburgh's port.

BOOK LIST

Baxter, Colin *Edinburgh* 1993.

Baxter, Colin *Portrait of Edinburgh* 1994.

Baxter, Colin *Edinburgh* Lomond Books, 2000.

Cant, Malcolm *Villages of Edinburgh* 2 vols 1986, 1987.

Chambers, Robert *Traditions of Edinburgh* 1824, 1868 (reprinted 1996).

Daiches, David *Edinburgh* 1978.

Gauldie, Robin *Walking Edinburgh: 25 Original Walks in and Around Edinburgh 2000.*

Gifford, J., McWilliam, C., and Walker, D. *Edinburgh* (Penguin Buildings of Scotland series) 1984.

McKean, Charles, with David Walker *Edinburgh An Illustrated Architectural Guide* 1992.

Youngson, A J *The Making of Classical Edinburgh 1750-1845,* 1966.

INDEX